OFFERING
to
THE WORCESTER WRITERS CIRCLE

who deserve much better
and much more

WRACK

WRACK

poems by
PHILIP WORNER

THE MITRE PRESS London
52 LINCOLN'S INN FIELDS, WC2A 3NW

Also by Philip Worner

EROS OR PSYCHE?
THE LITTLE MERMAID
ALL DREAMING GONE
FREEDOM IS MY FAME
THE CACTUS HEDGE
THE CALLING OF WENCESLAS

© PHILIP WORNER, 1971
SBN 7051 0084 7

*Printed in Gt. Britain for The Mitre Press (Fudge and Co. Ltd.),
London by Etherington Print Ltd., Crayford, Kent*

CONTENTS

City of God	7
Noël Algérien I	9
Noël Algérien II	10
Noël Algérien III	11
Noël Algérien IV	12
Canterbury	13
Rufus	14
Oh, who would cross the border?	16
To an Architect	18
Verses sent with Flowers	21
So easy for the young	22
Adonis	24
No gentler head	26
Dead prince of Severn	27
Advent	28
A cat may look	31
No Age of Princes	34
Wenceslas	35
The time to boast of love	41

"Rufus", "So Easy for the Young",
and "No Age of Princes"
have been read on
"Midland Poets", B.B.C.

CITY OF GOD

Peace on earth.
Though the Algerian moon
Ziggs the zagged roof of the "Tobaccocoop,"
... Acres of glass, and now a transit camp ...
The ack-ack guns are still:
A hundred miles ahead the German craft
Shift in the silt of the Tunisian sand.
So only dogs bark, by the slaughterhouse,
And it is Peace on Earth.
Now, after midnight Mass,
High on the hill, near S. Augustine's shrine,
(City of God, how far, how far!)
And dinner with the Marquise and her friends
... She'll think it rude I did not say goodbye;
For we, I know, at noon, are moving up ...
Now, in the shadow, through deserted streets,
Back to the Racecourse, derelict in mud,
And fellows sleeping underneath the stands:
In England now! In England at this time!
Will it be safe to cross the open square?
"No man can leave the camp without a pass."
"All service personnel will carry arms,
"And no one in the ranks go out alone."
I am alone, I have no pass, no gun,
How should I take a gun to dine with France?
Will it be safe to cross the open square?
Only the ghosts of beggars haunt it now.
But even in the acrid chill of night
Rubbish and rags start up with "Tangerines!
Buy Tangerines for chocolate, bully beef!"
And safe without a pass, without a gun,
To take this short way by the transit camp?

Nowhere a sound: today is Peace on Earth
Good . . . "Company, parade!"
Dark in the shadow of the Tobac wall,
Though opposite the hovels are dead white,
Troops from the transit camp are moving up.
The names strike at me, names I knew, I know;
Names that I learnt long since in English fields,
On English downland, deep in English woods,
In some lost summer by clean English streams,
Sic transit. Sic transit . . .
Sick! transit! . . .
Transit the youth and beauty of the world.

I search the faces by the factory wall,
But there are none I know.
So you, and you, and you may still be safe . . .
Down the hibiscus path of some fine house,
Where bombs have smashed at last the Roman stone,
I flee the laden company of death;
Into the orange groves along a rail.
Home in U.K.! Oh home in England now!
And peace again on earth, and peace on earth.
. . . Only the frogs, and now and then a rat.
And dinner and the wines of the Marquise,
And the intended honour of it all
To me, a common soldier, ranker, "Troops,"
Were perfect with the elegance of France . . .
Back to the unit, through the barbed wire fence,
Though I could sleep here, by the cactus hedge.
Back to the unit, and one day there'll be
No war, no arrogance, no slaves, no camps . . .
But peace on earth . . .
And even Ayrabs, à la Banque de France,
Home in the Kingdom.

NOEL ALGERIEN

His dogs kept soldiers of all kinds away

"They'll never miss you, down at the Château!
"Oh you must stay!" I saw the dark eyes shine,
"The long dark lashes fall. "As you well know
"They were all drunk . . ." "On your Algerian wine?"
"Already at midday. And we saw last year how,
"Although the Boche held Tunis, they were drunk
"Through all tomorrow too . . ." "My son, allow
"Men uniformed to drink!" "I may be drunk,
"If I take more of this." "But from our ride,
"From likes and hatreds shared, that will not be.
"This Christmas night the rebel by my side
"Shall represent the men who set us free."

    "How strange my son should ask you: till today
    "His dogs kept soldiers, of all kinds, away."

NOEL ALGERIEN

Where some chance serpent twines

"Late in the afternoon, among the vines
"Between the village and the mad Château,
"Or round high fields where some chance serpent twines
"Its tawny gold, secure, to sleep, below,
"The boy from the old Priest's house comes to look
"For rabbit food, for softer grass and vetch.
"Sometimes I help. So yesterday we took
"Enough to last all Christmas, without stretch.
"And later the old Priest invited me
"To lunch on Christmas Day; whilst to the lad
"I've promised that at midnight I will see
"Him serve at Mass." "But all that can be had:

"I'll take my sister's pony, you a horse . . . "
"You'll go to Mass?" "As Henri IV, of course."

NOEL ALGERIEN
Old stories in the stars

"Your father will be late, George, in Algiers,
"So take the keys, fasten the pens and sheds."
The sheep and horses and the tractor-steers
Into the lamplight turned their cumbrous heads.
You locked the yards; and, as we tried the bars
Across the building where the stills are kept,
We paused to trace old stories in the stars;
Unpromised in far huts the herdboys slept.
Back to the house through the hibiscus gate . . .
I saw your mother at the salon door
And as she said, "Help us to decorate,"
Mimosa heaped upon the parquet floor.

> A pause alone betrayed that fate replied;
> I had not used it since my mother died.

NOEL ALGERIEN
Since the star

Our lady-officer astounded France:
"My English voices, in the hushed midnight,
"Bid page and monarch through the snows advance!"
I waited for a Christmas that was white.
But after that, the universal Mass
Searched all the ages since the star was seen
To drag the lost from their most dread morass,
To set them free for what they might have been.
And on the steps, in scarlet and in lace,
The censer in those hands that had held mine,
He gave a worship time cannot efface,
Encountering, for a moment, the divine.

>   I stood beside the flowering aloe tree,
>   That Christmas Eve, and he ran down to me.

CANTERBURY

Does the solitary heron still
At dusk above your gaunt cathedral strain,
Into the sunset and towards the hill
Beating the winds that force it back again?
Remember that I watched him. Though in flight
He sees each gleam of silver in your streams,
As I in your eyes caught each gleam of light
And still shall see it through the mist of dreams.
So much you gave me that is always mine;
Nothing escaped me that had any pride,
And life and laughter shared have fed like wine.
The darkness deepens; you are by my side.

    Beneath, in the Cathedral, gold rays lance
    The grey bulk of a coffin cased for France.

RUFUS

Song waiting for guitar

He is King of the land
And he rides like the light
As he hunts the great deer
From the dawn into night,
From the dawn into night.

He is free in his woods,
He can race on the green,
In his forest no fear,
Only friends to be seen,
Only friends to be seen.

He has bright golden hair;
He can strike like a lance;
He is promised to wed
A pale princess of France,
A pale princess of France.

Slunk away in the town
The dark traitors now wait:
"He may ride out at dawn,
"We shall bring him back late,
"We shall bring him back late.

By a stream in his woods
He was shot through the side.
Only one friend rode up
To the King as he died,
To the King as he died.

So the traitors crept back,
And they "Murderer"! cried.
But the King's friend had gone
With the King as he died,
With the King as he died.

He was King of the land
And he rode like the light
As he hunted his deer
From the dawn into night,

From the dawn into night;

From the dawn into night.

OH, WHO WOULD CROSS THE BORDER?
Story for guitar

Born braw into a Scots band,
But if he crossed the border
He'd be Lord of all England
   And King of the two.

Stuart is a blood apart
And foes lie on the border,
Lurking to stab him to the heart,
   The King of the two.

He was Jamie VI of Scotland
But as he leaps the heather
He is First of all England,
   King of the two.

Good friends he finds in England,
Sped deep down from the border,
Sped away from Scotland,
   King of the two.

Good work he does in England;
There's peace along the border;
Two kingdoms work as one land;
   King of the two.

His foes temper a long knife
And secretly in London
Conspire to take the King's life,
   The King of the two.

His foes still cannot get him
Although they lurk in London,
His best friend will protect him,
   King of the two.

So first they mark the King's friend
Right down into the harbour;
Deep plunge the knife, deep, deep and rend
   The King of the two.

He was Jamie VI of Scotland,
But when he leapt the heather
He was First of all England,
   King of the two.

Who would be King of England,
Oh who would cross the border
To live alone in England,
   King of the two?

TO AN ARCHITECT

There is really something rather pleasant, almost fine,
On looking
New from tall windows of the gaunt grey Hall
To right and left
And forgetting the mistakes . . .
Even, perhaps, the Greeks
In temples that have perished missed
Perfection?
The mighty errors of imperial Rome
Time's hand has solved:
The immemorial Forum is a ruin;
The fastness of grim mediaeval lord
Moulded by wild rose and sweet English grass.

Admittedly here in the once fair Tudor city,
Working in black and white,
Mistakes of charm, despite
Development,
Persist (whose only hope is rapid
Rehabilitation in the States) . . .

Come back. Stand here.
Look from the Hall to left and right
And you shall see
Two gardens:
One walled, impregnable,
The Ladies' Bower
Of Chivalry,

Ringed from the world, remote;
Where entered
Nothing ruder than the rose . . .
Enters
Nothing ruder than the rose.

The other opening from (right)
Cryptic Vicenzean colonnade
And (left) (tintinnabulation)
Trim Tyrolean terracing,
(Terra, sing. Terra, terra sing!)
Sweeps to the little wood that's almost
Lost
Steep down towards the river, desperate
Across Royalist meadow to the bridge, the spire, and
Surprising now
In worlds so soon made
Dust
The great Cathedral
Elemental
Rock

And so for us
In time, in time,
Under lilac or laburnum or syringa
Moonlit under roses
Under love,
The years will ease the errors;
Gardens and buildings will collegial become one
Haunt, one home for mind and heart
To live for and to save . . .
That distant glass, a lake;
The school's green tower: the parkland's princely tree . . .
Let who builds more, let who builds anywhere build high
Build high, build high, build high
Build high
And leave live
The field
Below

Again, stand here,
Whatever arrogance of architects arranged this
Hall
None may deny it life,
None here forbid to help
Or hurt:
Here on this spot where singing birds were slain,
Here where summer lightnings lap your feet,
Here you can get your heart on Saturdays
Shattered a thousand times a night
Yet with the slightest touch,
A word, a smile . . . restored to
Beat
Again

VERSES SENT WITH FLOWERS

These tributes to the fine, free, fearless way
You worked with us and lived our common theme
Must fade, and age, and tremble, and decay.
And, tangible, sink softly down time's stream;
Though even they by your remembrance saved.
But countless in our sparrow-counted hearts
Shall live the happy chances you engraved,
Sunshadowed by your known, and secret, arts.
Down flowerless corridors of callous years
In gay print frock perennially fair
Unfailingly your slight form reappears:
You gently laugh with us at our despair.

> They do not need by fortune prince to be
> Who wander welcome in our memory.

SO EASY FOR THE YOUNG

It is so easy
To go up and wait at dusk along the by-pass
As searchingly, smooth, the great tiger lights
Speed up against the dark
And strike.
So easy, on the snow and ice of winter, even,
To stop the unknown driver
On the stark highway. The unknown driver
With eyes that one has never seen before
And does not look at.
Whose hope is destination and whose hand
Is destiny.

Even in appleblossomtime and cherry
Or when the scent of honeysuckle startlingly is
All one gets
From where a moment since fell back
The rose.
Or when the Hunter's moon goes down straight into the
Black
Track.

So easy at any time, winter or summer, day or night,
Convenient to oneself, necessitate by
Plans, hopes, fears, loves,
By things that cannot wait and things that can,
So easy to go
Out
From the familiar place,
Past the lighted windows,

And the arms that rise
To take a pen, to open books,
To push the debris back, to strike a match,
To switch the record on, to shut the door,
To fill the cups, the cup . . .

Alone and down the dusk,
Turning, slightly, the doomed head towards
The windows of your special friends,
Smiling, almost, to think of endless arguments
With them, with him, with her . . .
Now, at this window knock. Bright behind curtains.
You need only knock. Knock!
And he will come
At once beside you down as many miles as you can need
to go

No window but would open out to you.

Inconscient, independent, you go on
And it is dangerous now
It is always dangerous now
That turning set the course
Into the dark.
Equally for the fair,
Equally that head of brightest gold,
As easy for the head that's doomed and dark
So easy for the young
Casually, happily, an incident, taking with them
Merely just enough
For this weekend, that night,
So easy for the young at any time
To hitch a lift to death.

ADONIS

I let Adonis go

I let Adonis go
All summer long where cruelly
At the crude corner of the field
Ruin where even Venus will not seek
Some yards beyond the morning shadow of the broad
Warm arch
From foraging the wood raw rural
Arms had flung
Him
And forgotten
Forgotten they had seen and caught and hewn
A god within the tree
I let Adonis lie
I let him lie

All winter too

I dare not take him up
Implacable the master now is not
The gods
Is man

Better not notice as you pass the place
Better do nothing
Better let it be
Convolvulus vies vinculant with
Nettle
To envail the
Boy

Beneath the stars
Only the broad-grained chest
With the rough lion's paw of bark
Over the golden shoulder
Near the heart
Remains

No one comes happily at dawn
To wake him.

Never to wake Adonis
Never to wake Adonis
That is sad

Three times the summer gone
Three times the snow
Lies soft as chlamys on him
That the impudent wind will sometimes
Lift
Leaving stripped
The stripling oak

A little touch
The axe descended
He was gone

Had he been here now
I for I have loved you
Now I would have taken him to shelter into light
And I would have given him another name
Yours

To remember you
I would have renamed him
As on remembering him
I rename
You

NO GENTLER HEAD

No gentler head has bowed above a book.
No hand in writing less inferred of pain.
No love more generous than that quiet look.
No mind less scheming in the search for gain.
The ease of death would no-one less desire
Whose life was selfless work, and love, and play.
Though courage fail the slight form would not tire
Of fighting upward to the golden day.
But purpose is equated with a dream
When careless bearing all both good and bad
Life in its spate as fierce in spate the stream
Pauses for nothing least of all a lad

> Though sick with sorrow we our loss deplore:
> This heart knew breaking but shall break no more.

DEAD PRINCE OF SEVERN

Wings of a swan beat down into my sleep
And woke me through the still September dawn.
But you had drowned in Spring when waters leap
Fiercer than salmon in despair to spawn.
Down that green way that you compelled had passed,
My gentle lad, my perfect gentle friend,
Travelled so deep since I had held you last . . .
Deeper than arms, or life or love extend;
Deeper than stones that through slant waters slide,
Deeper than shadows when slow light is gone . . .
There, now, exultant, free, a prince in pride
Into the crystal sunrise mounts the swan,

> Serene. You would have longed for us to see
> Such strength in purpose to eternity.

ADVENT

Homing, home, homeheld
The candles of
Their Advent star that third
Night before Christmas
As I left old friends, gave more of warmth
Than myriad myriad candle power remote
In heaven.

Proofed by their welcome, constant through all cares,
By kindly "coruscation of converse,"
By the choice supper simply, sizzling served,
I gave no heed to frost
Outside on silent lawns until surprised
I saw it glittering harsh
Down moonlit bays.

Silent I moved down silent corridors.

Here just a week ago the lights swathed paths;
Here a humanity of voices called
Marking the hour
When individual minds contagiously
Relax into a brew
The better to work late into the night.

And seven nights are thronged with seven years
And seven years with seven full years again
As generations mingle like the stars...
So many friends;
Who should be lonely here?

I had to pass your room.
Beyond the door all the bright heads look up;
Brightest among them you.
I hear keen plans to set all life to rights
To win for all men freedom, justice, food,
Salvation spreading from this circle out
To hold the world.
These hopes fulfilled then how should Wulfstan win
Against S. Mark's, S. Mathew's, Army, R.A.F.,
How to play hooker Hamlet Hotspur Hal
How to race the universal tides.
Beyond them on your lighted desk the books
Await the midnight easier access of
Your mind.
Marking the places where your eyes must work,
On slips of paper orange, green and blue,
Roves
The royal initial of your name.

I knock.
(Oh here the poem lies).

The door is opened
And you are not there.

Not here.
The scouring of a week has not erased
The smell of coffee brews,
The perfume of the latest girlfriend's new
Make-up,
The sting of liniment
Of rugger kit that could be laid to dry
Along the pipes but would be better washed at once I think.
Nor muted your guitar

Dark, dark into the dark spur.

Then I remember how you never failed
However tired, however late the hour, however still,
To lift your arms and fix the golden time
When we shall meet again.

The Advent star

Leads

On

A CAT MAY LOOK

I no longer care what I say
Some ferocity, some power in that;
One can be wittier than one was,
And one can spit.

Having defixed my stare from prospects,
Hopes, promotions, recognition, fame, the future I
Can look the king through the face
And casually, carelessly, not searching;
Not striving subtle, not suave, not slink, not
Arching backwards in diplomacy,
With some contempt
Claw
On my right.

I wish I were in awe still of M.Ps.,
Of Undersecretaries, Ministers,
"Er, Prime Minister . . "
Lords, Earls, Dukes . . . That these all should
Come down to common parlance, common clay,
No intro. needed more than time of day,
"What do you think?" . . . "It seems . . ."
Colonels, Captains (Naval), Air Vice-Ms.,
Retired . . . The gorgeous uniforms
No longer Them . . . to mow the lawn,
Take tea, prune hybrids,
"Dear, shut the window, please,"
And reprimand only the Press. Their words
No longer power of life or death to men;
As facile, feline, futile as my own.

No terror now to face Captains of games
Nor Chairmen, Presidents of Circles, Clubs, Societies . . .
What does it matter what one says to them?
So easy to fawn anything you like.
Councillors' speeches of whatever Party hold no
Forestalling vision . . .
Obsequies only slip from Mr. Mayor.

Lecturers, Professors, Principals, Vice-Chancellors . . .
Regius and Regent laced in gold . . .
So what the hell?

Not difficult to scratch the Vicar now,
Rectors, Archdeacons, Deans,
Archbishops, Monseigneurs . . . their glories
Like as bubbles
Evanesced;
The residue, in slippers, is the man.

Where now their words?

Four letter words have lost their secret power,
Their vigour vanished into virulence,
Worn flat so flat by station, dosshouse, pub,
By football terrace, prison, showers, school . . .
To general impotence.
Anything at all may now be said
Yard after yard the pallid words
From printing presses universal unifoisted news
Cocooning all the heartbeats of the world.

No need to be a tiger to do that;
Any lesser cat can equal all;
So easy and so slick . . . so caged a
Cat.

  And yet and yet
  Yet when this golden head,
  This fair, this dark, this liferefulgent head,
  This cropped, this curled, this rough, this silken head,
  (It cannot, cannot know),
  Roves within a half-inch of my lips,
  This soft, this harsh, this sweet, this acrid hair . . .
  This light, this dark, this golden golden hair
  Stirs at my indrawn breath,
  Still predator . . .

Then let me speak, then let me stalk the skies
Leash lightnings for my words
Spin back lost years from through the swirling stars
Rage Vulcan of the sunset
Great angel lord of darkness
Swanspirit of the dawn

NO AGE OF PRINCES

This is no Age of Princes; common man
Whatever honours may be heaped upon him
Must from the imperious head, the curlèd hand
The diamond smile, the patron's nod, the trim
Caress, the elegance, the pride . . . refrain
Even the actor now must equalise;
Statesmen be "Mister" who would titles gain;
The priest affect no concord with the skies . . .
Alighting from your car you must not stalk
As though disdaining plebs-discarded stubs;
Meeting with people, you are free to talk
With any accent that's approved in pubs.

  Princes of Fortune can come down to earth
  But what of those who Princes are by birth?

WENCESLAS

This square is ours;
We had a country once.
Mountains and forests, valleys, villages
Where Spring came late and could not stay,
Home and a ray of happiness that fled.

This statue's ours;
We were a nation once.
Let us go through;
We lived together, friends in little homes,

Suddenly hopeful, suddenly laughing, singing, almost
Free,
Saw truth again, kept faith.
All crushed except this statue.
Let us through.

This day is ours;
We had a future once.
Let us go through;
We have the right to live the day it died.

Why all these guards?
Why all these bayonets?
Why all these nightmare tanks?
Let us go through.

A country that's one square,
A nation that's a statue only,
A future that's one solitary day:
Some threat in these?
How can these things fight?
Square, statue, day: a danger to the State?
Let us go through.

We cannot harm you, cannot hit you even.
Our only metal is a few small coins.
The flowers? The candles? Violence? Assault?
Such fragile offerings to our vanished past?
Let us go through. Move back around the square.
We have no bombs, but if you think we have
Press them in on to us. Safer round the square.
Safer to let us through. Through in an hour;
The crowd dissolved. The thousands of us gone;
A vast illusion: folk of Wenceslas.

If not the men, then let the women through.
Let at least the women place their flowers.
Men and boys move back. Back!
The women through.
Give them your flowers and candles;
Let them crowd a moment round the King;
Weep for our past a moment . . . held in a silent square.
The women through! Let just the women through.
The women cannot hurt you; let them through.

The girls then, just the girls!
Come, comrades; just the girls. Look at them, now.
The nation may be dead; the girls are lovely still.
Make way for beauty; let the young girls through!

A mother too, perhaps.
Yes and a mother; who has lost her son.
His mother should go first; let her go through.
And silently the young girls go with her.
And silently the young girls go with her.
You're young enough to have your mothers, too.
Let this one mother through with all the girls.
Handbags and bombs to boy-friends!
Carry nothing with you except flowers;
Flowers and the candles; they won't last a day.
Parade tomorrow and you'll find no trace.
Nothing to show a flock of girls went through.
The girls, the girls! Come forward all the girls!

These cannot be men. The uniform
Conceals a race of robots, spawned by tanks.
In single file then let us all go through.
Just let us walk through quickly one by one.
No one would risk a bomb.
A legend winding through a city square,
Not to return again.
Through to the statue but not even kneel
Let flowers and candles fall.
Stretch out a hand to touch the past
Electrically one moment and then on.
Let us go singly through;
People lined out in grief can do no harm;

In that way clear the square;
Off duty then, you guards.
We could stay here all night and keep
You here. Let us file through:
You're free before it's dark.
In single file then, down the bottleneck
Our good Czech wine! Line up behind this kid;
Let him go first. Quick everyone;
Meet on the other side.
(Silently the line of sorrow forms;
This innocence, the seed of Wenceslas . . .)
Afraid that tears have power?
Not even if they fall upon the blades.
Lift up the bayonets and let us through.
Well, split the guard, if you'd feel more secure.
Bring both halves round in two sharp lines of steel.
Much like a guard of honour? We'll think of it
As two high tension wires to touch would kill.
Suspicious of the candles and the flowers?
Pass all the flowers and all the candles back!
Mother, we'll put yours very carefully over there;
High on the windowledge above the street.
They will last longer there. Tanks will not crush them
Nor the hooves of guards.
Yours specially, we'll put yours specially
On that high window-ledge facing the King.
Frame all the square with flowers!
Now empty-handed let the people through.

Will any girl go first? Then single file.
That's easier. They're bound to let one girl. The girls in file.

They would not harm the girls one by one;
Cain had no sister.
(That was killed, you mean). The girls in single file!
Look everything we've brought is piled up now,
Masses of flowers and candles round the square
And spilling down the side-streets into dusk.
Promised: we'll leave them there.
And when we've gone; when we have seen
This mother and the girls file giftless past their Saint
We'll clear off;
Leaving the flowers a carpet for your tanks.

Try further down.
This one looks human;
Under the helmet hides a human face;
Even a guard must want a human face;
Must want a child born with a human face;
Our future once appeared with human face.
Man, let your sisters through!
In simple single file; one by defenceless one;
They've nothing in their hands;
Just one by one. (But this face, like the others,
(Turns to steel.

(Another wave of steel moves up.
(The crowd recedes, leaving a bitter space;
(The sunset lays on them a purple grief;
(Like beasts the great tanks shift upon the stones
(Crushing slowly out the scent of flowers;
(The girls move vomitively back;
(Thousands of candles gleam around
(The sick-bed of the square.

(A boy moves forward;
(Still the crowd recoils.
(Alert the bayonet glitters;
(But a glaze obscures the young guard's eyes.
(The boy smiles.
(Then slowly bends his head to see what make of steel
(This is. The golden hair is blown against the blade).
And you can speak our language? Claim our blood?

Don't let him be killed! Make him come back!
(A man steps up behind him. Runs
(His finger on the fine bare flesh
(Between the jacket and the jeans.
(Others crowd round him now).

Let fifty of us through! Let twenty . . . ten!
Let me alone.
Let me go through alone. Search me,
Strip me if you want; let me go naked through,
One solitary friend for all our past.

Let the boy go through!
The boy go through . . . The boy through!
The boy through! . . . The boy through!

Stamped on this bayonet I see one word:
"Traitor" (Blade boy vest flesh
(Thrust). "Traitor".
(Lost).

Not flowers, not tears, not blood . . .
Only the snow can cover
Wenceslas.

THE TIME TO BOAST OF LOVE

The time to boast of love is after death:
When I, then you, are gone where cannot reach
Injustice nor the subtlest serpent breath
Of cruelty. Then shall they know us each
With each for lovers equally. Then I
May glory that your lips touched me, touched me;
Mine on your every slightest hair would lie.
My lips that loved you loved untiringly
Your every . . . hair. Since . . . , you.
No . . . hair concealed. Loved everywhere.
All day I watched your eyes from green to blue:
All night, dear heart, dear heart, my angel care.

    Still you turn . . . to me. Your fierce arms
    Reach out to keep me from an age that harms.